A PRACTICAL GUIDE TO
REINVENT YOUR LIFE IN THE POST COVID WORLD

DARSHAN M

To get the maximum out of this book, it would be best to read it once. Then come back and read individual chapters, answer the questions and do the exercises in each chapter.

This book would not have been possible without the patient proof reads and edits by Sal, Shobit, Ruella, Shivani, and Vijeta for the illustrations.

First Published by Notion Press 2020
Copyright © Darshan M 2020
All rights reserved.
ISBN: 9798687137393

The views and opinions expressed in the book are the author's own and facts reported have been verified to the extent possible. The author is not a doctor or a medical care provider and has no expertise in diagnosing, examining or treating any kind of physical or mental health conditions. The exercises and information given in the book are for reference only and to be used under professional guidance. They are not offered as a replacement or substitute for professional medical advice. The author, publisher, distributors make no representations or warranties with regards to the completeness or accuracy of the information in this book.

This book is sold is being sold subject to the condition that by way of trade or otherwise, be lent, resold , or hired out, or otherwise circulated without the author's prior consent in any form of binding or cover other than in which it is published and without a similar condition including this condition being imposed on the subsequent purchaser.

For the love of my life, my wife Shivani, who has been an anchor through all of my storms and a lighthouse through my dark days.

FOREWORD

An ode to life!

Life is a very funny phenomenon.
One can live it in one continuum.
Or one can live it in phases.
Or one can live it in ups and downs, highs and lows.
It depends entirely upon how one wishes to live it.

This book is more autobiographical and less management jargon. It is best read as a continuum, for as far as I know Darshan, he is living it as one. The truth lies in each word he says as he has been there, done that, learnt this and experienced that. This comes from someone who has possibly gone through more vicissitudes of a single life than most of us can ever imagine. Yet he seems to have no serious grudge but instead moves on as tomorrow is a fresh dawn.

I have personally learnt a lot from Darshan in his various roles as consultant, mentor, ideator, creator and friend over the years. And the lasting impression I carry is of a man who is calm and smiling, not as if to accept the present but because he is planning for a better future.

This book is more like a novella and less like 14 individual chapters. That will help the reader arrive at the bigger picture that Darshan wishes to paint for all of us.

The bigger picture is about accepting ourselves with our vulnerabilities as much as our strengths. It is about failing as much as about succeeding. It is about exploring as much as about mastering. It is about restlessness as much as about stability. It is about teaching as much as about learning. When you see life as a large canvas, you cannot fill it with just a finite set of objects that you are familiar with; the canvas needs to have its fair share of intrigue and the unknown.

"Trade your cleverness for bewilderment" as Rumi said and Darshan quotes. That to me is the essence of living a full life, for it is so precious.

This book is about life after the pandemic rather than about how to survive it now.

It is about how to prepare for the 'fresh dawn' as Darshan always does. It is about focusing on all that will help us not merely survive beyond the pandemic but embrace the world with open arms.

I am reminded of an incident during World War II when the Allied forces were mapping bullet holes in the aircraft that returned to base to determine areas for reinforcements. The Romanian mathematician Abraham Wald, then teaching in Columbia University, asked them to focus instead on the aircraft that did not return and reinforce areas that had no bullet marks on the returning aircraft!

We tend to suffer from a phenomenon called "survival deviation" where one focuses on things that have survived rather than on things that have not.

This pandemic is teaching us many a lesson on focus, adaptability, empathy, adventurism, curiosity and celebration. As the famous cardiac surgeon Dr. Christiaan Barnard once said, "The business of living is the constant celebration of being alive."

Dive right in.

Avik Chattopadhyay
Co-Founder Expereal, Columnist at the *Economic Times*, *Business World*, Autocar India, *MxM India*, *Fast Bikes* and *Mint*.

"YOU NEVER KNOW HOW STRONG YOU ARE UNTIL BEING STRONG IS THE ONLY CHOICE YOU HAVE."

BOB MARLEY

PROLOGUE

They have lifted the enforced lockdown across the world, yet how many of us are continuing to live in a constant state of mental lockdown? My thoughts are echoing from the recent and sad demise of the Bollywood actor Sushant Singh Rajput. Like everyone else, it pained me to imagine what must have driven him to do what he did. From the outside, he seemed to have everything that is not within the reach of millions. He seemed to be living a dream. My family is yet to come to terms with it despite us never knowing him or ever meeting him. I felt a similar knot in my belly when the founder of Cafe Coffee Day took the extreme step. I had met Mr. V G Sidhartha quite a few times and was in awe of his achievements and his humility. I often quoted his example of remaining simple. Never did I imagine an end like that, and it still pains me to even think of it.

I would be lying if I said I never entertained such thoughts. There have been some extremely weak moments in my life, when I too considered suicide. I thank God for helping me claw my way back from those dark moments. In reality, taking one's life is easy, it takes just one moment of madness, but 'making' one's life requires a lot of self-love, faith, gratitude and perseverance.

It's very hard to know what is happening inside anyone's mind and often external appearances are deceptive. In this lockdown most conversations I had with friends, colleagues, young executives and even seasoned entrepreneurs seemed to be filled with anxiety, fear and in many cases helplessness. From millionaires to the homeless, everyone is affected by this pandemic.
I am inspired to write this book to help anyone who feels lost, confused or distressed in these surreal times. I hope you benefit from my learnings, experiments and experiences. Always remember you don't get to choose when you are born or when you die, but you surely get to choose how you live. My wife always says she is

her favourite person. Live well and love yourself 'first'.

This book may appear to be about reinvention, but in reality it's a book about life. The immortal truth about life is everything is changing continuously. As you read this paragraph, there are cells being born and cells dying within you. As you grow older everything changes from your external appearance to your internal outlook. A life well lived, is a life where you are evolved and reinvent yourself over and over again.

When I was a young kid, I dreamt of being an archeologist. I picked up numismatics as a hobby and loved treasure hunt based movies like the Indiana Jones Series. I never ever thought I'd have a career in media or sports or fashion. I was just plain lucky to be in the right place at the right time. I have made a few good decisions and plenty of blunders too. Everything I am today, I owe to regularly re-skilling and reinventing myself.

I want you to look at this book not as a self-help book but rather as a practical guide to reinventing yourself. It's not a book just for the pandemic period; it is a book for every time you feel stuck in life, or at work, or at school.

And remember if you don't put what you read to practice, it's pointless to read in the first place. Remember the famous quote by **Bruce Lee:** "I fear not the man who has practiced 10,000 kicks once, but I fear the man who has practiced one kick 10,000 times." So read a couple of times but practice a zillion times.

© Darshan M
www.darshanm.com

Foreword	5
Prologue	11
Introduction	17
Evaluation	25
Learning	39
Digitisation	60
Identify Your Niche	64
Brand Building	67
Virtualise Your Life	72
Automation	76
Cockroach Mode	80
Build Mind Colonies	84
Mindset	87
Fear	89
Goal Setting	96
Art Of Being Happy	102
La Familia	110
Epilogue	113
About the Author	115

1. INTRODUCTION

"IN THE MIDDLE OF EVERY DIFFICULTY LIES OPPORTUNITY"
ALBERT EINSTEIN

A few months ago, I met a fellow entrepreneur for coffee. In the midst of the wide-ranging conversation he asked me a very fascinating question: "Which of the top ten companies in the world do you think will exist in twenty years' time?" I instantly told him the ones that are able to keep **reinventing** will survive and the others will perish. We all have witnessed many famous brands disappear like Kodak, Nokia, Blockbuster, etc; and if you examine them thoroughly, they were not poor businesses or poorly run institutions. They just did not maintain pace with the evolving world. Most executives are busy making innovation happen for their consumers but neglect to change themselves. If you think about it, we all change constantly. Who we are today is not who we were a month ago. Our knowledge has changed; our outlook has changed; even our expertise has changed. Yet we all follow the adage, "Don't fix what is not broken." So what really happens is someone from the outside comes and breaks it for you. You then either react and try to salvage the situation or you crumble and die. **The smarter ones are the ones who will break it down themselves and rebuild better versions now and then**.

The pandemic has inspired me to write this book because never before has this generation been compelled to learn and reinvent itself on this scale. We have lived through Y2K, Dotcom Bubble, The Gulf War, 9/11, the Sub-Prime Crisis, SARS, and EBOLA epidemics, but this time it's different. You know that the world will never be the same again. Some things will change forever. It's one of those "once in 100 years" kinds of event. The global spread of coronavirus disease (Covid19) has been unprecedented in the modern world. The pandemic and the subsequent lockdown have pushed the global economy towards an impending recession. Stock markets have gone through some of the worst collapses since the 2008 financial crisis.

The closest parallel one can think of would be the 1918 Spanish flu pandemic. The 1918 flu affected about one-third of the world's population. Conservative estimates put the death toll between 20 and 40 million, while some estimate it near 50–100 million. On the last count the covid19 virus has infected over 12 million people globally, with over 500,000 succumbing to the pandemic. The pandemic is causing destruction of the magnitude you witness in a war-like situation. It's not just health but the economic debacle that is causing anguish. Isolation, social distancing, economic catastrophe and extreme changes in daily life can lead to an epidemic of clinical depression.

Millions of jobs have been lost so far, and thousands of small businesses have wound up in a short glaring span of a few months of lockdown. Many enormous companies will go bankrupt in the Travel, Tourism, Leisure, Retail and Financial sectors.

The world as we know it will change forever as we officially now live in the **VUCA** world.

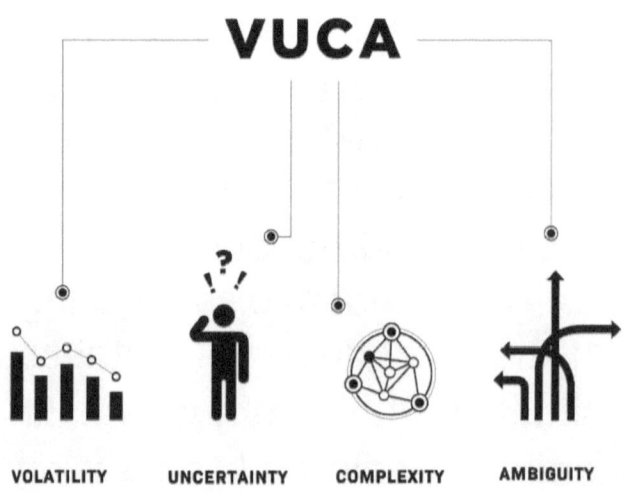

VUCA stands for **V**olatile, **U**ncertain, **C**omplex and **A**mbiguous. The VUCA management principle for crisis management recommends you focus on Vision, Understanding, Clarity and Agility. This is the time when you are expected to go back to the drawing board and revisit why you started in the first place. Understand your core competence, focus on the primary market, and be agile. **I always recommend "First Principles Thinking", which talks about deconstructing enormous problems to basic elements and building them back from the ground up. Many eminent leaders follow this theory first promoted by Aristotle. The concept is all about dismantling the assumptions and focusing on the pure essentials.**

While the problems are all real, it's not all doom and gloom. The emotional, physical and fiscal crisis that will come in the post covid era will need us to reinvent the way we think, work and live. If you want to survive and thrive in the new normal, you will have no choice but to reinvent yourself.

We regularly update the software of our mobiles and laptops, but when was the last time we updated our internal software? When was the last time you took stock of your life? When was the last time you checked on your priorities? When was the last time you took a journey inward? When was the last time you reskilled yourself? Many of us stop our education once we leave college/university and are ill-prepared for the modern world. The only thing constant in this world is change; yet we stick to our old proven methods while facing this constantly evolving world.

This crisis could be an opportunity for all of us to reinvent our lives and our businesses. It's time to reinvent the way we think, live and work. As a young kid, I remember a framed quote on my dentist's wall that read,

"Problems are opportunities in working clothes."

Yes, this giant problem could be the giant opportunity you have been waiting for all your life. You have been so busy with work, traffic, deadlines, and social media that you never took the time to figure out what you wanted from your life!

When was the last time you sat and reflected and analysed your life, your passions and dreams? This unplanned lockdown is allowing all of us to do just that. This is the opportunity to reinvent your life to what it deserves. But remember it will be a lot of hard work too. After all, the quote reads, "opportunities in *working clothes*."

The problem is that we do not value what we have and instead criticise what we don't have. It is not about being locked in our homes but being happy we have a home to keep us safe. We have to learn to value our strengths, our talents and our blessings. Remember, the fire within you is much stronger than all the fire that surrounds you. Use this book as a practical guide to reinvent and rise. The following chapters will give you clear step-by-step instructions to reinvent and rebuild your life.

"IT IS OUR CHOICES, HARRY, THAT SHOW WHAT WE TRULY ARE, FAR MORE THAN OUR ABILITIES."
— J.K. ROWLING, HARRY POTTER AND THE CHAMBER OF SECRETS

2.
EVALUATION

EVERY DECISION YOU MAKE REFLECTS YOUR EVALUATION OF WHO YOU ARE.
- MARIANNE WILLIAMSON

If you have picked up this book, you have already taken the initial stride towards reinventing your life. So congratulations on taking the first step. The most critical step on this journey, is **self-evaluation**. It is important to gauge and revise your actions to ensure they are as efficient as they can be. Evaluation can help you determine areas for growth and help you realise your objectives more successfully.

Wherever you go, you carry with yourself all your thoughts, feelings, beliefs, your stories, experiences and all your perspectives from your life. When was last time you retested your perspectives to evaluate if they are still true for you? Are they still serving you? Let us begin with first evaluating ourselves. If you are not aware of where you stand, how will you decide where you want to go and where to begin?

So how does one self-evaluate? **It can start with an authentic record of your life. You can break down your life down into the many parts: Social, Emotional, Physical, Educational, Financial, etc**. One easy step is to use the popular **Wheel of Life method** created by Paul J Meyer.

You need to draw a circle and divide it into eight sections like in the image below.

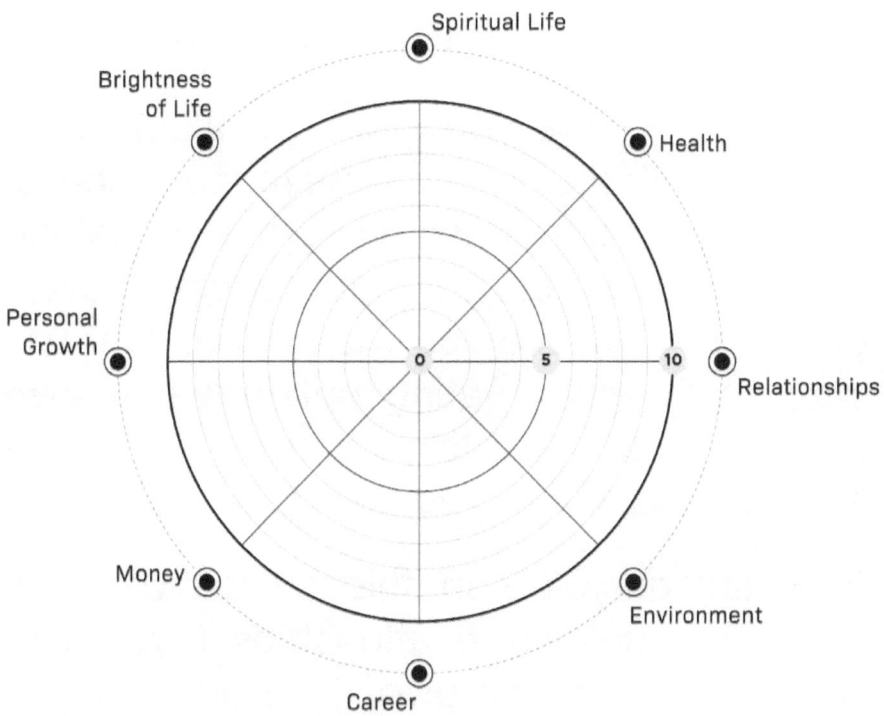

Each of the eight zones in the circle represents a slice of your life. You self-assess each zone of your life by giving it a score between 1 and 10, with 1 being unhappy and 10 being super happy.

Be forthright and provide an accurate value that will illustrate your satisfaction with each facet.

The eight aspects of your life include:

1. Health - Here you should evaluate how you feel about your appearance, fitness, energy levels, nourishment, sleep, habits, etc. Be honest about where you stand today and not where you wish to be. Just because you enjoy eating out and you love beer, you cannot rate your diet a 10. Honestly assess where you stand.

2. Relationships - In this sector you can judge the quality of relationships in your life. Relationships include friends, family, spouse, neighbours, colleagues, etc. All relationships are a two-way stream not just how you feel.

3. Environment - This sector is where you evaluate the physical space like home, neighbourhood, surroundings, city, country, etc. Compare where you planned to be with where you are. Do not accommodate; nor should you fantasise. Be realistic given your circumstances while still being unemotional as you rate the quality.

4. Career - So here don't think about income; that is another sector. Instead focus on your career area, passion, job satisfaction, growth trajectory, social status, time investment, business, progression, etc. Try to understand how happy you are with what you do for a living. Do you feel excited about what you do? Do you look forward to the work you do?

5. Money - This section is where you think about how much you earn, how much you spend, savings, etc. Again, don't be unrealistic but practical. Think about how much do you need and not about how much you want!

6. Personal growth - I urge you to spend some time thinking before filling up this sector. This is often a neglected area, so ask yourself if you have enough time for self-improvement. How satisfied are you with your personal growth—your education, reading, learning new technology and skills, etc.?

7. Brightness/Quality of Life - This is the qualitative side of your life. Think about some activities to make your life brighter. Think relaxation, entertainment, hobbies, sports, travel, art, music, culture, etc.

8. Spiritual life - This is where you bring in God, your religious activities, your spiritual activities; think of meditation, yoga, reiki, social service, etc.

This self-assessment will mark the beginning of your journey to reinvention. This is a crucial part of the journey so please spend some time doing the evaluation. If possible, get evaluated by your close friend, colleague and spouse who may share some perspectives that may be oblivious to you.

TIPS FOR SELF-EVALUATION

Ask yourself hard questions on your strengths, weaknesses, habits, lifestyle, etc. And give impartial answers. This is not an office appraisal so you need not try to prove anything to anyone. You don't even need to share the self-evaluation sheet with anyone. If you're uncomfortable don't show it to your friends or family. But please don't lie; face the mirror and tell yourself the truth. You cannot start the journey based on a lie.

Document your achievements. Sometimes we forget what we have achieved so write them down. The survival instinct makes our brains remember negative experiences more than positive experiences. I recommend you maintain a **success journal** to document every minor success in your daily life. Another fun thing to do, especially for kids, is to keep a **happiness jar**. Every night, write down a small note on what made you happy and drop it in the jar. At the end of the year, open the jar and count your happiness for the year. Trust me, you will be glad you did this exercise.

List your problem areas. Do not give in to the temptation to brush aside the areas that need improvement. If you are not clear about the scope of improvement how can you make any progress? Like you spent time writing about your achievements, spend an equal amount of time listing areas for improvement.

While doing the assessment, focus on your mindset too. Think about your comfort zones, your beliefs and traits. If the need arises, you can make a fresh sheet just for the internal evaluation. It is critical for you to understand why you are here before making any plans to go elsewhere. A lot of the decisions we make in life are not because of circumstances but because of the way we are wired deep inside. So the evaluation of our beliefs and internal traits is critical.

And remember you have to repeat this exercise at regular intervals. Try to do it every quarter or at least twice a year. And at surreal times like the Covid19 pandemic please evaluate again, as this once-in-a-lifetime event deeply affects our lives.

As a part of your self-evaluation, ask yourself some life-changing questions. I call them life-changing questions because sometimes these questions will alter the course of your life. This pandemic has given all of us enough time to sit down and reflect. Pause for a moment and look at your life from fresh angles. Ask the important questions that will help you understand yourself better.

LIFE-CHANGING QUESTIONS:

Am I proud of who I am?

Ask yourself are you what you always wanted to be or have you lost your way? Do you feel proud of what you have become? Are you still keen to be what you wanted to be? Who are you? What do you care about? Do you matter?

Where will I be five years from today?

If you continue on this path where do you think you will end up five years from now? What changes do you need to make if you are not happy with where you will end up? Do you need a change in direction, effort or attitude? What are your worries for the future? What are you scared of? Have you done anything of late that is worth remembering?

Have I got my priorities right?

Where do you spend your time? Do you give enough time and attention to your loved one? Do you think your folks will live forever? When was the last time you spent quality time with them? Are you busy or do you make time for friends and family? What have you learnt from your mistakes? Are you holding on to something you need to let go of? Are you putting enough effort into your relationships? How would you live if you knew you were dying?

Have I grown?

Every mistake you made taught you something. Have you learnt from them or are you still making the same mistakes? Have the failures strengthened you or made you weaker? Have you become better or bitter? When did you last push yourself out of your comfort zone? When was the last time you showed some kindness to a complete stranger?

Am I surrounded by positive people?

You are the sum of the people you hang around with. So ask yourself, do the people you spend time with encourage you? Do they motivate you to be a better person? Do they make you smile? How many friends would you trust your life with? Who has helped you the most in your life? Remember birds of the same feather flock together, so if you are not surrounded by happy, positive and successful people you are not likely to be happy or positive or successful.

What am I taking for granted?

This is a crucial exercise. During this pandemic most of us will have asked this question. Have you taken life for granted? What about your health? And your job? Have you taken your relationships for granted? Do you value what you have? During this pandemic did you feel they locked you up or were you grateful to have a safe place called home?

What is my genuine passion?

What are you passionate about? If you had all the money you wanted in your life what would you really do with your life? Does anything set your soul on fire? What do you love the most about yourself? What makes you wake up every morning? Will you pay to do something that you are not doing now? Is there anything you will do a deal with the devil for? Remember a life without passion is not a life worth living. And we all have passions; some pursue them while others leave them behind. And those who leave them behind never lead fulfilling lives. So spend some time answering these questions.

I cannot explain enough the benefits of this self-evaluation exercise. Introspection and reflection are all about taking the power away, from the way you have been conditioned, away from your beliefs, away from society, and bringing your focus of control, back to where it belongs, within you. I will end this chapter with a quote from the famous Chinese philosopher **Lao Tzu**: "***Knowing others is intelligence; knowing yourself is true wisdom. Mastering others is strength;*** 3.

3.
LEARNING

"THE BEAUTIFUL THING ABOUT LEARNING IS THAT NOBODY CAN TAKE IT AWAY FROM YOU."
B.B. KING

Learning is the process of gaining new understanding, knowledge, behaviours, skills, values, and choices. Learning can be Cognitive; which means knowledge-based, or Affective; which is emotion-based, or Psychomotor; which means action-based. Humans, animals, plants and nowadays even machines display capabilities to learn. Growing up, I was invariably told to learn subjects, games, concepts etc., but never was I taught 'how to learn' or 'why to learn'.

When I glance back at my life, I cannot recall using much of what I picked up through formal education. It has been the experiences that have taught me my most valuable teachings and supported by my reading. It was the nasty experiences that were the finest teachers. The pleasant experiences don't develop you enough, so all of us need to have a few unpleasant events in life in order to grow. That reminds me of the ancient African proverb, "**Smooth seas do not make skilful sailors.**"

I credit all my prosperity and disappointments in my career to the two crucial questions "Why?" and "Why not?" We, humans, start learning even before we are born and keep learning till we die. So it's comfortable to deduce that we are alive as long as we continue learning. I guess learning is equal to breathing; stop either of the two and you will perish. Never mistake education for learning. If you think some fancy certificates or titles are the end of your learning, then you will fade away and become redundant. The American Author Grant Allen said, "I allowed no schooling to interfere with my education." They credit this quote to Mark Twain even though Grant Allen published this 20 years before Twain. Only when you investigate will you learn facts that didn't exist earlier!

THE ART OF UNLEARNING

"**Learn to unlearn.**"–Benjamin Disraeli.

Did you know that quote from Mark Twain was actually from Grant Allen? We accepted what we were taught and ended up assuming that was true. The initial step to learning anything is unlearning. Now, why should you unlearn before learning? I will refer to the Old Chinese Zen teaching, "Empty your Cup". The story is about a scholarly man who called on a Zen teacher to inquire about Zen. As the Zen teacher talked, the learned man interrupted to communicate his own opinion about this or that. Finally, the Zen teacher stopped speaking and served tea to the scholarly man. He poured the cup full then kept pouring until the cup overflowed."'Stop," said the learned man. "The cup is full, we can pour no more in".

"Like this cup, you are full of your own opinions," replied the Zen teacher. "If you do not first empty your cup, how can you taste my cup of tea?"

Especially now in these times of the pandemic, you have to unlearn in order to adapt and reinvent your fresh life. Achieving a balanced life is key. It requires lots of things, but most of all it requires an empty cup. You need to challenge your preconceived notions at every turn. Engage with fresh ideas. And always keep an open mind. Keeping your cup empty will help you do just that.

Another reason for unlearning is sometimes what we know is not automatically correct. Remember, every kilometre you travel in the wrong direction is a two-kilometre mistake. I am reminded of the renowned Mark Twain quote, "It ain't what you know that gets you into trouble. It's what you know for sure that just ain't so."

When we're growing up, we absorb a lot of messages from parents, school, society, religious leaders etc. on what is 'good' ,'bad,' 'success', 'failure' or 'correct'. We also pick up habits and beliefs based on our adventures along the way. Some may have been coping techniques that helped us survive through a tough period, but all of them remain with us long after.

If you want to reinvent your life and embrace fresh ways of viewing the world then you need to first unlearn all limiting mental models, outdated internal narratives, and beliefs that you've developed throughout your life. And if you don't first unlearn your old beliefs, you will not be receptive to novel ideas and fresh opportunities. Buddhist teachings speak about the concept of "knowledge that links together". We learn something new by first linking it to something we already know. Information connects by linking it to locations within a familiar environment. This is a common practice used by memory champions to remember colossal amounts of data. Most of the time, this is useful and helps us navigate through significant amounts of learning. Every once in a while, when we are attempting to learn something new, this unconscious linking creates issues and hinders your learning. Therefore, most of us go about demanding that reality conforms to our ideas, rather than the other way around.

I have come across many smart people who could have been rich and famous but failed to live up to their potential because they could not unlearn and relearn. You will also know people around you who refuse to listen to any fresh ideas, opinions, and methods. They believe what they know is the only correct method and everything else is wrong. **The people who make it big in life are lifelong learners**; they learn from everyone—seniors, juniors, janitors, everyone.

I am often told by many that unlearning is very difficult. And I concur; yes, it is difficult but not unattainable. Think of it like moving from India to the USA. You have to get used to the new ways of living, new culture, alternative methods and even driving on the wrong side of the road (wrong for an Indian but right for the American). You will experience some teething issues, but eventually you learn and become good in the alternative ways. Empty your cup and you are always ready to learn.

If you are amenable to admit that all you know need not be the right or the only successful approach, then learning any new skill, language, technique, etc. should be a breeze.

Unlearning is unpleasant for most people. Finding out something you thought you knew was false will confuse you. Yet that is normal. So how can we ease the process of unlearning?

Tools and Tricks to Help You Unlearn

1. **Never procrastinate** - The first thing our mind wants to do is to avoid anything unpleasant. People often procrastinate because they're afraid of failing at the tasks they need to complete. This fear of failure can promote procrastination in various ways, such as by causing people to avoid finishing a task or by causing them to avoid getting started on a task. So every time you feel like postponing, deliberately push through and make headway.

2. **Try unfamiliar experiences** - Trying out fresh experiences that you never tried before helps your mind become accustomed

to accepting novel ideas, thoughts, formats, and ways. Now and then try new food, try to enjoy new music or even learn an extra dance step. When your brain gets used to trying unfamiliar experiences, it becomes comfortable with the unknown and this is when you become more open to unlearning and learning.

3. **Cultivate curiosity** - This habit will serve you not just in unlearning but in your entire life too. Be curious and chase mysteries with just the idea of learning new answers. This will teach you how to learn to let go of prejudices. I have lived my entire life with this mindset of curiosity. I always want to know why and how something happens. My experiments range from the garden to the kitchen. Not every curious experience leads to happy or good results. I remember putting a spoonful of cocoa powder in my mouth once, thinking it would taste like chocolate and I can feel the awful taste to this day.

4. **Prove yourself wrong** - Another well-proven method is to ask yourself if you

could be wrong and then research an argument to prove yourself wrong. This does two things: First, it exposes your mind to a lot of fresh information and, second, it gets your mind used to looking at unique perspectives. And you are more likely to accept your arguments rather than be told off by someone else. Doing this all the time usually annoys friends looking for advice. Thus, I end up giving them advice from both sides by speaking for and against on any topic. And I do this because any decision you jump into without looking at the facts and comprehending the impact will always be wrong. So make it a habit to look at both sides of the argument before deciding.

5. **List your beliefs** - This is an exercise all of us need to do often. Think of it as the spring cleaning of your mind. Make a list of all your beliefs and ask yourself if they have served you well and if you are where you deserve to be. And once you give yourself the honest answers, you will know which ones to keep and which to let go of.

The Learning Toolkit

"TRADE YOUR CLEVERNESS FOR BE-WILDERMENT." - RUMI.

So now that I have prepared your mind to receive the new knowledge, let's begin the process of learning. Before you embark on a journey of learning, you need to remember the right approach to learning. You must learn to understand. And never confuse learning with formal education. True learning is like diving into an unexplored abyss in that it involves a process of first undermining the things you thought you had learned. You need to let go of all the facts, ideas, and theories you learnt to get to something deeper. And remember learning is not a spectator sport. You have to get involved and act.

I remember meeting many double master degree holders for whom education was a hobby or maybe even an addiction. For these kinds of people knowledge is like an addition to their collection. They may buy a lot of books and even read most of them but implement none of the lessons. This approach of knowing but not doing is not learning. Genuine learning is a quest that never stops until you find the answers. And like it's described in ancient Indian philosophy, it's cyclical and continuous. You learn, unlearn, and learn again.

I would like to believe I am a student for life and will always continue to keep learning. Everything I have achieved in my life is because I never stopped learning and always lived with a curious mind.

Attention - The first step to a journey filled with a lifetime of learning is to pay attention. You may notice the fastest learners in the world are kids. And the fundamental difference between a child's approach to learning and an adult's, boils down to focus. The ability to pay attention and be present is the first step to learning. Unlike kids who can focus on an activity for hours, adults scatter in multiple distractions. If the mobile phone notifications, thoughts about pending bills and other constant interferences disrupt your learnings, then you cannot learn anything. Listening can be empathic listening, selective hearing, attentive listening, pretending to listen or even ignoring. Most people do not listen to understand, but we listen intending to reply. Don't respond to someone's problem with a solution until they ask for it. Just listen to understand how they feel.

Fail - The second step is to be comfortable with failure. This is a very important step because if you get scared of failure you will shy away from even attempting to learn at the very first slip-up. Also remember sometimes losses can be more valuable than wins. A healthy attitude will help you draw wisdom from every experience. Like I mentioned earlier, it is my failures that have taught me the most. The great Thomas Alva

Edison said, "I have not failed. I've just found ten thousand ways that won't work."

Curious Mind - The third step is to develop a curious mind. The biggest problem is they train us from childhood not to question what they teach you, while in reality we should teach every child about the five Ws and the H. They are, Who, What, Where, When, Why, and How. The answers to these questions are the basics in information gathering or problem-solving. If you can cultivate this habit of trying to ask these questions before accepting any fact you will become a true learner.

Forgetting Curve - Like the learning curve, the next step is re-reading. Most of us never re-read a book we have previously read. Research has validated that re-reading has hordes of benefits. So make a habit to go back and relearn what you already have learnt and you will notice newer, subtle aspects that you missed the first time. Therefore, the top performers in the world always do the same thing repeatedly. As they say, to become a kung fu master you need not learn 4000 steps, you need to learn a few steps 4000 times. Repetition is the only path toward perfection. Research shows that 48 hours after you learn something new you forget it.

Linking - Another effective tool to learning is emotional connections. We are all emotional beings and when you link information with an emotion, you develop it into a stronger memory. All of you will have a song that takes you back into a memorable moment. You will notice that consuming some food or a certain scent can take you back in time. That is because those flashes are information combined with emotion.

Teach – And, ultimately, the best way to learn is to teach. The beauty of teaching someone is that it does not just require you to first learn and master the subject but also digest it. Only when you have understood can you break down the lesson into small, understandable bits, thus improving your cognition and growth.

Mentor - And one last point before we close this chapter is to get a mentor. Have you noticed all the biggest sports stars in the world have coaches? Does Nadal or Federer need someone to teach them how to play tennis? In business and in life, you need a mentor, someone who has been through these roads before you. A mentor/coach will provide motivation, guidance, and emotional support.

Celebrate the differences - Most often we don't want to hear an original opinion other than ours. This attitude limits our ability to learn and grow. Always remember the more diverse views and ideas you get the better your view of the problem becomes. Learn to appreciate the various views and embrace them to become better at finding the right solution. Exceptional leaders always get the team together to brainstorm rather than dictate a solution.

And don't forget learning is continuous. It is like breathing—you stop doing it and you will die. Before we close this chapter, I would like to impress upon you a fact about learning. Never mistake learning for just input; input coupled with an output is genuine learning. So if you just continue reading and don't implement what you read, you get a false sense of competence. This is just an illusion because you are never competent without having implemented the teachings. If you watch a motivational video, read a book or attend a seminar but don't put into practice the learning then you will have learnt zilch.

To understand this better, let us break down input and output. Input is when you consume knowledge through audio, video, text or in person. The output is assimilation, reflection, and implementation of the input. So how does one master this aspect of learning?

First, remember the ratio of time between input and output should be 1:3, which means you spend three times the time in implementing your lessons.

The first step of output is assimilation. You must make notes when you are inputting knowledge. If you are reading a book always keep a highlighter with you to underline and highlight the key takeaways. If you are watching a video or a webinar or listening to a podcast, keep a notepad with you to capture key takeaways.

The second part is to reflect on those notes. See how you can implement them into your daily life and work. Schedule it into your calendar.

The next step is to implement the teachings. Remember, a lousy action is still better than no action. Once you have scheduled it, do it. Remember, it's better to have embarrassing results than no results.

The last step is to share it. The best way to master anything is to teach your learning to others.

If you can do everything I have listed in this chapter and continue to stick with it you will be well on your way to becoming a master of your destiny. Learning has to be continuous and a way of life.

'REFLECTION IS ONE OF THE MOST UNDERUSED YET POWERFUL TOOL FOR SUCCESS'
RICHARD CARLSON

THE ENEMIES OF LEARNING

Information overload - Take in information in small chunks. Most of us get overwhelmed with too much information. Try not to multi-task and stay focussed on one topic at a time. I can tell from experience that biting off more than you can chew will only cause indigestion. Learn to have small portions and once your digestion powers increase you can start consuming larger portions. Just like you learn to crawl before you run, start slow but be consistent.

Digital distraction - In continuation, do not let your mind get scattered. We have too many sources like mobile, social media, etc to keep pulling us in different directions. For instance, while trying to write this chapter on learning, I kept getting distracted with my phone until I had to switch off the mobile to focus on writing. This is where mindfulness comes to your aid. Mindfulness is the ability to focus all your energy and attention to the task in hand. You can develop this skill through meditation, yogic breathing exercises, etc.

Digital dementia - This is the latest and fastest-growing disease in the world. All of us have learnt to outsource our brain to computers and smartphones. How many phone numbers do you remember? When was the last time you tried to recollect knowledge from memory, instead just rely on Google? You have forgotten basic maths. One wonderful trick is to get back to the good old days. Take notes with pen and paper, try to recollect data from memory and not Google. And please do your basic maths in your mind and not on your phone's calculator.

4.
DIGITISATION

"ONCE A NEW TECHNOLOGY ROLLS OVER YOU, IF YOU'RE NOT PART OF THE STEAMROLLER, YOU'RE PART OF THE ROAD."
STEWART BRAND

A quick look back at the past industrial revolutions will teach us that organisations and individuals that do not evolve fast enough will be less competitive or even obsolete as they face disruptions in every industry.

The pandemic is forcing all businesses and individuals to embrace technology. Even the fence-sitters have no choice but to digitise their lives. The post-Covid19 era will have an economy shaped by new habits and regulations based on increased hygiene. We will see reduced close-contact interaction and tighter travel restrictions. The current disruption will change how you eat, work, shop, exercise, manage your health, socialise, and spend your free time at an unprecedented rate of change.

All the high-touch industries are now gearing up for a future of low-touch economy. So you will witness an influx of more digital enabled business. How prepared are you for this new economy? Do you have the skills and expertise to survive and thrive?

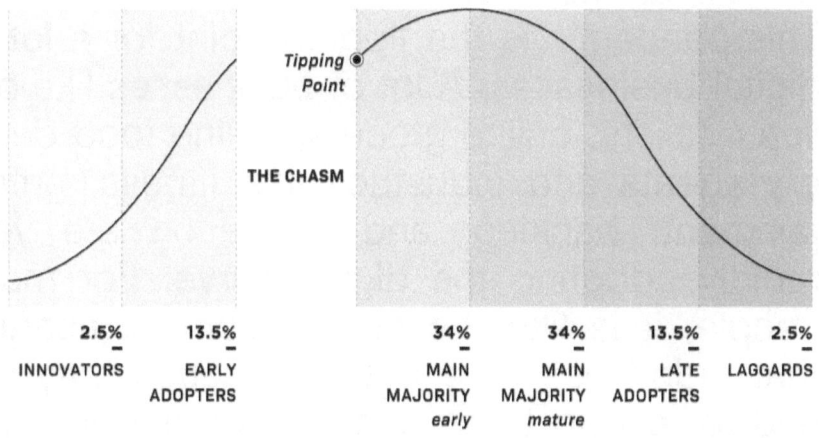

I am sure all of you have heard of the phrase "tipping point". In sociology, the tipping point is described as a point in time when a group rapidly and dramatically changes its behaviour by widely adopting a previously rare practice. The image demonstrates the normal tipping point.

Usually, when a new technology product or service is introduced, it needs to cross the tipping point before the majority of the population embraces the same.

However, in these surreal times of the pandemic, the whole population is forced to adapt to new habits, technologies and ways of life. This pandemic is the tipping point for a lot of digital businesses. A lot of businesses like online retailers, online grocers, online food delivery agents and industries like fitness, entertainment, banking, and education are very rapidly adopting the digital curve. For many people, it is like the old telecom companies that didn't use fibre optics because they still had to recoup the investments made into the copper wires. I still know a lot of people who will not change hardware till it gets obsolete and they are forced to upgrade. I find is hilarious to see requests for fax numbers in contracts to this date.

Personally, I have been quite there and thereabouts. I did use the regular cab hailing, food delivery, OTA and e-commerce apps, but this pandemic has gotten me hooked on e-learning in a big way.

When you think about embracing a digital life, it begins with you. Instead of asking, "Is there a reason to do this online?" we should be asking, "Is there any good reason to do this in person?"

From outsourcing to micro sourcing, e-commerce to organising your wardrobe everything exists on your mobile, but we still do many things the old-fashioned way and now will be forced to adopt this at a rapider pace.

In the following chapters, I will share clear steps to embracing a digital lifestyle that will help you reinvent your life and work.

5.
IDENTIFY YOUR NICHE

"ALWAYS REMEMBER, YOUR FOCUS DETERMINES YOUR REALITY."
GEORGE LUCAS

I read somewhere a long time ago, "There is no secret formula to success but there surely is a secret formula for failure. It is trying to please everyone."

I believe in this formula and post the pandemic it is going to be more relevant than ever before. The world will have less space for generalists and will seek out more specialists. As we go deeper into the digital world we will soon realise that knowledge is not power. Knowledge actually is free, but insights are the real power. There are over 2.5 quintillion bytes of data produced every day. A quintillion has 18 zeroes if you are wondering. Google performs 3.5 billion searches each day. So the information is on overload. A quick search will show you how to do anything from cooking a simple meal to making a bomb. So the last thing the world needs is another jack of all and master of none. If you want to survive and thrive in the new world you have to reinvent yourself as a specialist.

There are many ways to find your niche, but in my experience the easiest way is to find the core of who you are as a person. Your core can be defined as who you are and what your values are. It's difficult to comprehend so I have made a diagram for your easy understanding.

Think of it as the centre of your skills (what you are good at), talent (what comes naturally to you), passion (what gives you joy), causes (what change and impact you want to make to this world) and finally market (where is the demand and what can make you money). At the core of all this is who you are and that should guide you to finalise your niche.

6.

BRAND BUILDING

PRODUCTS ARE MADE IN A FACTORY BUT BRANDS ARE CREATED IN THE MIND.
WALTER LANDOR

A brand is not a name and logo. A brand is not only for companies. Even you as an individual can be a brand. In my various talks, I usually ask a volunteer to go outside the class and pick a pebble/rock and bring it to me. I then ask the class how much someone would be willing to pay for this rock. I try to sell its virtues of being a great paperweight and strong and unbreakable, etc.

Usually, there are no buyers and sometimes out of pity someone offers five bucks. I then ask the class to imagine that this rock came from the Berlin Wall. During its demolition, the company that was given the contract to break the wall was also given the task to dispose of these rocks. I tell them I have a certificate of authenticity and this is a proven piece of history. Now suddenly people are willing to pay 500 bucks for the same rock. I then ask the class, "What if this rock was brought down from the moon by Neil Armstrong and was the only piece of lunar rock outside of NASA?" And then suddenly it's worth millions. In these stories you realise the brand value of the rock changed according to the story attached to it. So what is your brand value? What will people think about you when they hear your name?

Today, building a personal or company brand is so easy thanks to the digitisation of the world. It is so easy to get your story across with the advent of the internet. In the old days, only the press could print, only the broadcasters could broadcast. Today, the power is in your hands. Anyone can write a blog that will be read by millions; anyone can shoot a video and upload on YouTube to reach millions. And all these are for free.

The first step to building your brand is to build your consistent digital footprint that reflects your true personality and your specific niche. Remember everyone from prospective employers, business associates, and clients to potential life partners will first research you online. The surveillance economy is here to stay. Everything you say, do or see online is being observed and will be used. So the first step is to review your digital footprint and bring it into order. Make sure it reflects your passion and your aspirations.

The second step is to create content. Write blogs, articles on LinkedIn, stories, post videos etc. based on the niche you want to be known for. Most of us are happy forwarding someone else's WhatsApp message or reposting on social media. Create your message that reflects your niche, your personality, your story and your voice.

Do a Google search of yourself and see what crops up. Do you like what you see? If not then fix it. Get yourself a good LinkedIn page, manage a consistent image across all your social media and even build a personal webpage that speaks about you as a whole (not just work but your passions, causes, etc.). Remember two things when you embark on building your digital brand. **Be authentic and be consistent**.

Why am I asking you to build your brand? **The future is not of big brands, the trust deficit, will ensure people will trust peers and micro-influencers**. You may have noticed that your news consumption has moved from a newspaper and news channel to social media and WhatsApp. Who do you think has a greater influence on your life, Barkha Dutt or your WhatsApp group moderator? You are regularly influenced by friends and micro-influencers every day and the power will only increase in the future. If you don't become someone people want to hear from then you will be one amongst the audience. Be heard to be a brand.

I personally believe investing in your brand is the most important investment you will ever make. So pay attention to what you say write and where you will be seen. How people perceive you is the actual reality and not how you perceive yourself.

7.
VIRTUALISE YOUR LIFE

"MOST OF US SPEND TOO MUCH TIME ON WHAT IS URGENT AND NOT ENOUGH TIME ON WHAT IS IMPORTANT."
STEPHEN COVEY

Most of us have not yet utilised the full potential of the digital ecosystem. This pandemic has forced us to adopt and use a lot of tools we never tried before. Now that you have learnt new ways, make this your new normal. Don't yearn to go back to the old ways.

First, adopt remote working. If you are a business owner, explore getting rid of your fixed office and convert all employees to remote employees. If you are an employee, try to convince your organisation to let you work from home at least for a few days a week. Many of us learnt the joy of spending time with loved ones instead of grinding it out at a cubicle and spending hours in traffic jams thanks to this crisis. Many start-ups I know have paid the price of having a fancy expensive office. This crisis has taught us all we can do without an office, or foosball tables and sleeping pods. Money spent on these unproductive but cool items is lost forever. I have seen universities now adopting more remote internships and remote program delivery.

Secondly, outsource everything and anything you are currently doing. From virtual assistants (VA) to virtual coaches the internet has all the experts and helping hands you need if only you are willing to switch. The physical world only creates limitations. If you find a VA in another city or even another country why do you have to adjust to what's available locally? You may find a marketing advisor in another city for far less than what is available to you locally. The easy way to plan the outsourcing is by first evaluating where your maximum time is getting spent and within those areas choose the ones that surely could be a better use of your time. The second aspect is to see if the areas are not your area of expertise and in that case outsource. Then look at cost factors; if it can drastically reduce your fixed expense, again outsource.

And finally, embrace the gig economy. The future is all about freelance experts who you hire (or get hired) to do specific tasks/projects and not full-time jobs. Anyone who has managed a team will know that even though your team is in office nine to five or sometimes nine to nine, it does not mean they are working all the time. On an average, an employee will do productive work one to two hours; the rest of the time goes into social media, mindless browsing, taking calls, chatting with colleagues, tea, snacks, lunch breaks and sometimes even job hunting. So why not hire experts to do the job and not break your head managing people? This may not be possible for all industries and sectors, but if you think hard, you will see how you can build efficient teams with a mix of full-time and freelance experts.

Ask yourself what you are still doing the old way. Can technology help increase efficiency? I would any day choose technology to do most of my work so I have more time for my family and my passions.

8.
AUTOMATION

"WHAT YOU DON'T DO DETERMINES WHAT YOU CAN DO."
TIM FERRISS

Now that you have started this journey of utilising the true power of technology, it's time to automate. Automation is the next logical step once you have begun digitising and virtualisation. Many of us are still unaware that most emails we receive are not sent by real humans but software programs. Most chats you have today with company agents are actually with **chatbots**. Today, there are tools to automate everything from emails to SMS and Whats-

App. Large brands have always been used them, but now they are accessible to all of us.

When I started my career in sales, I used to collect birthday and anniversary details of all my customers and ensure I sent them wishes diligently. It was all old-school pen and paper, no computers, no smartphones, etc. Today, it's so easy to fire-up a software program that will make you seem like the most thoughtful person on the planet. The software customises the communication and even gives you insights into who opened, when, etc.

Advertising and marketing today is all built around smart automation. For every scenario, there are rules and specific actions that are pre-programmed. For example, in my e-commerce business Deivee, if a potential customer visits and leaves without shopping from our store, they get a reminder email the next day. This is usually followed up with an additional push notification on their desktop a few days later. Cookies ensure that wherever they go –

Facebook or any website – they see our ads. This prompts them to come back and browse again. All this happens without any manual intervention. Customers get emails on their birthdays; follow-up emails to customers who have not visited the site are sent automatically.

I have automated everything from order processing to the outsourced warehouse getting the order and it's fulfilled without me having to do anything. My journey with automation has moved to the next phase of experimentation. I have moved my e-commerce business from 20 full-time employees to zero employees. This pandemic has forced me to shut my office. And now I run a leading yoga lifestyle e-commerce company with zero employees and zero office. I hire virtual interns to help now and then. And I don't see myself going back to the old ways anytime soon.

If you are in the marketing or customer relationship space, you cannot function without automation. Every large brand does it now and you should too. As an exercise make a list of repetitive work you do and explore using tools like Zapier to build rules and automate today.

Remember everything has a cost, even time. The time spent doing something unproductive is actually eating into the time you could have been productive.

9.
COCKROACH MODE

"HE WHO WILL NOT ECONOMISE WILL HAVE TO AGONISE"
CONFUCIUS

Yes, you heard that right, "Cockroach mode". First, let's understand cockroaches; they have been on planet Earth for 320 million years and their survival skill is legendary. They can eat anything to survive—fruit, leather, paper, skin flakes, hair, dead insects and even soiled clothing. They can live for a week without their head and can die only from lack of water. They can live a month without food and are expected to survive a nuclear explosion.

Now that you understand how smart cockroaches are let's understand "cockroach mode". This is survival mode. This mindset is one of resourcefulness and not waiting for resources. I come across so many young individuals who seem to be forever in waiting. They have a bunch of excuses from lack of time to money, resources, expertise, network, etc. The cockroach mindset is about making no excuses and getting the job done however you can. You make do with what you have and continuously improvise as you go along.

Of late there has been a lot of talk about cockroach start-ups in the Silicon Valley. These start-ups, unlike unicorns (billion-dollar valued start-ups), don't focus on valuation but profitability. Post this pandemic you will see the roads littered with carcasses of unicorns and, you guessed it, the cockroaches will be feeding on them. If you want to thrive in this crisis period, you need to embrace cockroach mode. In poker terminology, "It's not about waiting for a better hand but playing with the hand you have been dealt."

Think of yourself as a leader of an expedition to Mount Everest. If there is a sudden avalanche and you are trapped in the middle of nowhere, you need to lead your team to safety. What would you do? Are you going to sit and wait for help or are you going to improvise and figure ways to survive and get your team back down to safety? What would you do? If you don't cultivate this mindset, you will not be able to reinvent yourself. Every great leader has to reinvent himself/herself continuously as they progress towards greater heights.

Some key characteristics you need to build if you want to reinvent yourself with cockroach mode are as follows:

1. **Frugality** – Don't waste money on luxury and instead only on bare essentials during this period. Survival is key and you will always ensure you and your business will survive for long periods.

2. **Flexibility** - You have to be highly adaptable to all situations. Remember Darwin's theory was not about the fittest species

surviving, it is the most adaptable species that will survive.

3. **Humility** - A cockroach has no ego. You need to be able to leave your ego at home and get moving forward. If you have to ask an ex-employee of yours for a job so be it.

4. **Perseverance** - In a boxing match you don't lose because you fall, you lose when you refuse to get up. You need true grit to keep getting back on your feet and giving it another go.

5. **Awareness** - You need to be aware of everything happening around you. You cannot afford to be running with blinkers; you need to be aware of threats and opportunities that may even be behind you. If you have flown in a plane you'll know they tell you the nearest exit may be behind you and yet everyone still only looks in one direction.

10.
BUILD MIND COLONIES

"ALONE, WE CAN DO SO LITTLE; TOGETHER, WE CAN DO SO MUCH" HELEN KELLER

The future belongs to those who can build digital tribes. The power of the internet lies in its communities. Whether it's a WhatsApp group or a Facebook community or even your Instagram following your influence will determine your worth in the future. So how does one build a community around themselves?

I am reminded of the adage I learnt when I first joined the media industry. "Great content will lead to great communities and with great communities comes great commerce." So it is essential to have great content that revolves around your brand. However, building and retaining a digital community isn't as easy as it appears to be. It requires consistent effort on your part. These are the main guidelines to follow:

1. **Content Is King** - Always remember it's the quality of your content and not the quantity of your content that matters. Your content should be useful, helpful and interesting to the audience. Always put yourself in the shoes of your audience and ask yourself how you can add value.

2. **Listen** - I often tell my friends, "God gave you two ears and one mouth." What does it mean? It means you need to learn to listen twice the amount you speak. If you are to build a good community, then you need to listen to the audience—what they like, what they want and what they care about. They will tell you what you need to write, shoot or record. Social media platforms give you meaningful insights into your target audience in the analytics sec-

tion. In addition to the analytics read all the comments and feedback.

3. **Maintain Consistency** - Consistency in both quality and regularity is key to keeping the attention of your community. Remember we live in an age of mega distractions. So if you don't maintain regular contact you will lose your audience to other sources of information and entertainment.

4. **Collaborations** - Another important way to build the size of your community is to collaborate with other influencers and content creators. Bring in outside speakers/experts to regularly keep adding value to your community.

11.
MINDSET

'YOU DON'T NEED A NEW DAY TO START OVER, YOU ONLY NEED A NEW MINDSET'
UNKNOWN

In the following chapters, we will cover the mindset required to bring alive the true reinvention within you. Everything starts and ends with your mind. The power of the mind is the most powerful tool in your possession. Every thought you put into your mind is instrumental in creating the life you lead.

Researchers in America were shocked to find that people who watched the news coverage of the 9/11 attacks displayed similar patterns of PTSD (Post Traumatic Stress Disorder) as those who had suffered in the attack. Just repeated exposure to bad news caused depression, anxiety, etc. The wrong media consumption led to increased risk in both mental and physical health (including lower immunity and heart-related diseases).

So, in effect, if you want to reinvent your life you need a new mindset. You need a bulletproof mindset. The mind is a vast subject and could fill a book on its own. In the following chapters, I will give you insights into the three most crucial areas you need to focus on immediately to get results.

12.
FEAR

"OF ALL THE LIARS IN THE WORLD, SOMETIMES THE WORST ARE OUR OWN FEARS."
RUDYARD KIPLING

The dictionary defines fear as "an unpleasant emotion or thought that you have when you are frightened or worried by something dangerous, painful, or bad that is happening or might happen."

In reality, fear is a natural emotion and a survival mechanism. When we confront a perceived threat, our bodies respond in specific ways. Physical reactions to fear include sweating, increased heart rate, and high adrenaline levels that make us extremely alert. While the chemical reactions are the same for every person, the emotional response varies from person to person.

All the chemical and physical changes that happen in your body are designed to help you survive. So everything it does, like increase adrenaline, etc., is to make us more alert. But in reality how many of us are more alert when we are engulfed in fear? All psychology studies speak about the natural response of "fight or flight"; however, no one speaks about freezing in the moment.

I have had all three experiences in my life. I have run away from situations and I have also become alert and fought my way out of situations, but most often I find myself in limbo. The fear just cripples me and I am not able to even think straight. While I should fight or take flight, I find myself doing absolutely nothing despite knowing what to do. I don't know how many of you can relate to the feeling of being helpless, the sinking and the suffocation.

I have noticed that when I just take some deep breaths and start focusing on my breathing I start calming down. Once in a calm state of mind suddenly all the problems seem less ominous than they did just a moment ago. You start noticing the options and the solutions seem to appear out of thin air.

So the first step to reinventing your life begins with us first learning about our own emotional and chemical reactions to various situations. Can you guess how many emotions a human can experience? It's around 34,000. So while it's hard to understand all 34,000 distinct emotions, we can learn how to identify the primary emotions and act accordingly. The six most basic primary emotions that serve as the foundation for all others are joy, sadness, disgust, fear, anger and surprise.

Here are a few exercises to manage fear and anxiety. Remember anxiety can affect you physiologically too and even lower your immunity.

(i) Breathing Exercise

When you're feeling anxious, you might notice that your heart rate and breathing gets a bit faster. You may also begin to sweat and feel dizzy or lightheaded. When you're anxious, getting your breathing under control can relax both your body and mind. Ensure your exhalation is longer and slower than the inhalation. Repeat these long, slow breaths till you feel your heart rate calming down.

(ii) Visualising

When you start to feel anxious, sit in a quiet and comfortable place; think about your ideal place to relax. While it can be any place in the world, real or imaginary, it should be an image that you find very calming, happy, peaceful, and safe. Make sure it's easy enough to think about so you can return to it in your mind when you feel anxious in the future.

Think of all the small details you'd find if you were there. Think about how the place would smell, feel, and sound. Envision yourself in that place, enjoying it comfortably.

Once you have a good picture of your "happy place", close your eyes and take slow and regular breaths in through your nose and out of your mouth. Be aware of your breathing and continue focusing on the place you've imagined in your mind until you feel your anxiety lifting. Visit this place in your mind whenever you feel anxious.

(iii) Relax your muscles

When you feel anxious, you might notice strain or tension in your muscles. This muscle stress can make your anxiety more difficult to manage in the moment you're experiencing it. By relieving the stress in your muscles, you can usually reduce your anxiety levels.

To quickly relieve your muscle tension during moments of anxiety:

1. Sit in a quiet and comfortable place. Close your eyes and focus on your breathing. Breathe slowly into your nose and out of your mouth.

2. Use your hand to make a tight fist. Squeeze your fist tightly.

3. Hold your squeezed fist for a few seconds. Notice all the tension you feel in your hand.

4. Slowly open your fingers and be aware of how you feel. You may notice a feeling of tension leaving your hand. Even-

tually, your hand will feel lighter and more relaxed.

5. Continue tensing and then releasing various muscle groups in your body, from your hands to your legs, shoulders and feet. You may want to work your way up and down your body tensing various muscle groups. Avoid tensing the muscles in any area of your body where you're injured or in pain as that may further aggravate your injury.

Managing fear and anxiety is the first step in reinventing your life. Only when you conquer fear will you be able to focus on what needs to get done.

13.
GOAL SETTING

"IF YOU WANT TO BE HAPPY, SET A GOAL THAT COMMANDS YOUR THOUGHTS, LIBERATES YOUR ENERGY AND INSPIRES YOUR HOPES."
ANDREW CARNEGIE

The great Russian Novelist Fyodor Dostoyevsky once said, **"The mystery of human existence lies not in just staying alive but in finding something to live for."**

Everything in your life first begins in your mind. If you want to go anywhere in this world, you need a map and a plan. If you have not sat down and asked yourself where you want to be in five, 10, 15 years you are just wandering around aimlessly.

I can stress the need for proper goal setting for a fulfilling life. I wonder why they never teach this at school. A life without any goal is not worth living. A life without ambition will be monotonous, boring and uninteresting.

In the recording of The Strangest Secret, Earl Nightingale says, "Have you ever wondered why so many people work so hard and honestly without ever achieving anything in particular, and why others don't seem to work hard yet seem to get everything? They seem to have the 'magic touch'. You've heard people say, 'Everything he touches turns to gold.' Have you ever noticed that a person who becomes successful tends to continue to become more successful? And, on the other hand, have you noticed how someone who's a failure tends to continue to fail? The difference is the goals.

People with goals succeed because they know where they're going. It's that simple."

In the last few years, I have personally made it a point to ensure the first thing any new hire does is goal setting. Once you define your goals you find clear purpose and direction. Your goals are the ones that make you get out of your bed every morning. It is the goals that keep you motivated when you slip and fall. It's this purpose that defines the quality of your life.

Often a lot of young people come and ask me if it's okay to change their goals. I say, "It is okay and, actually, your goals have to change over time. You cannot have the same or similar goals all your life." As described by Abraham Maslow in his book *Motivation and Personality*, a person's goals and desires change over time. It moves from basic physical needs to spiritual desires over a lifetime.

So how does one set goals? And how does one achieve the goals?

We have all heard of George T Doran's S.M.A.R.T. method of goal setting where he defines that all goals must be Specific, Measurable, Attainable, Relevant and Time-Bound. Since then there have also been many more structures like PURE (Positively Stated, Understood, Relevant, Ethical) and CLEAR (Collaborative, Limited, Emotional, Appreciable, Refinable), etc.

You can choose any of these structures if you need to. It's really easy to get caught up in someone else's goals or aspirations for you. So always ask yourself, "Is the goal I am setting something I want?" Think hard about what you want before you decide to chase it. Remember Aesop's Fable: "Be careful about what you wish for, lest it comes true." Once you are clear on your goals, here is what I recommend if you want to achieve your goals.

1. The first and most important thing in goal setting is to write the goals on paper. There is something about writing down your goals; it kind of already sets you in motion towards them. And

once written ensure you see and read them every day.

2. The next step is to create a to-do list. Every single day write down a list of things you need to accomplish in that day and that week. And every day make sure you strike off the completed tasks. This will also build your confidence and give you a sense of accomplishment with the progress you make.
3. One point to remember while writing your goals is to be specific. Break it down to the last denominator. For example, instead of writing, "I want to make money," write down, "I want to earn/save 100 bucks next week." You will notice that, all of a sudden, your goal and the route to achieving it will become clearer.
4. Then comes my favourite part—daydreaming. I cannot explain the benefits of daydreaming. Spend time every day imagining what your life will look like once your goals are realised. The power of visualisation has been widely writ-

ten about. After all, your life is the sum of what you think about the most.
5. The next and very important task is to consciously leave your comfort zone. Comfort zones might feel safe, but they can also stagnate growth. So push yourself to adopt new challenges and try new things. And if you fail, celebrate it, as it's proof you tried. Remember success is a journey, not a destination.
6. And lastly, learn to celebrate every small win. It may seem premature to pop the champagne, but these small wins, when celebrated, will build your motivation and confidence.

14.
ART OF BEING HAPPY

> "IT ISN'T WHAT YOU HAVE OR WHO YOU ARE OR WHERE YOU ARE OR WHAT YOU ARE DOING THAT MAKES YOU HAPPY OR UNHAPPY. IT IS WHAT YOU THINK ABOUT IT."
> **DALE CARNEGIE**

The first step to reinventing yourself and being successful is actually to be happy. Yes, you heard me right; if you are happy you will be successful. Most people have it backwards; they think they will be happy once they succeed, while the opposite is true. **Happy people attract more happiness, success and even luck**. The art of being happy is one of the most sought-after and also the most misunderstood concept. Most people are unhappy because they look for happiness everywhere except where they can find it within themselves. Happiness is a state of mind. And it can be found only when the mind is not agitated or in a state of turmoil. Listed below are simple and easy steps to rediscover happiness.

1. The first step to being happy is to look inwards. Philosophical and theoretical literature on happiness is abundant in India. Ancient texts and scriptures like the Vedas, the Upanishads and the Bhagavad Gita have explored the nature of happiness, and the insights gained from these writings are still relevant to modern people. Bhagavad Gita (verse 5.21) mentions that, "He who is unattached to the external world and its objects, and is attached to the inner Self, will attain supreme happiness, which is everlasting." Happiness lies deep within us, in the very core of our being. Happiness does not exist in any external object but only in

us, who are the consciousness that experiences happiness.

2. The second step is acceptance. Unlike the Gregorian system of calculating/measuring time, the ancient Indian philosophy believes that everything in life (the good times and the bad times) is cyclical. It is believed that happiness and sorrow are two sides of the same coin and they will come in cycles. From early childhood, I have grown up celebrating Ugadi (south Indian New Year) with an offering of neem and jaggery. We are made to eat this neem and jaggery mixture to learn to accept the sweet and bitter moments of life in equal measure. So one has to accept that life will not always be a bed of roses; you will receive your share of thorns along the way. You should accept them both without resenting one or craving the other.

3. The third step is being mindful. Mindfulness is the psychological process of purposely bringing one's attention to experiences occurring in the present moment. It's the same that is taught in yoga, Vipassana

and all Buddhist teachings. The art of being present one hundred percent in everything we do is not as easy as it sounds but neither is it as difficult as people make it out to be. We live in a day and age where we are easily distracted. Since the invention of the smartphone, people can't seem to have a silent meal or a focused meeting or even a family get-together without being distracted. If you can master the ability to be present in every activity, you do then you will find so much happiness and peace in your life.

4. The next step in achieving happiness is in service. **'Lokah Samastah Sukhino Bhavantu'** is a Sanskrit prayer (or sloka). It has been used for many centuries to invoke greater states of compassion and peace. Often said at the end of yoga practices, it's an invocation for personal and collective peace. "Do unto others as you would have them do unto you" may be the closest Western equivalent. Yet, the impact of this ancient mantra is far grander than simple human kindness. To be happy and successful, first serve others. There is great joy

in bringing joy to others. Seva is often defined as "selfless service," service with no expectation of reward. True Seva is a way of life, an inner attitude of giving. So go out and volunteer, help someone and share your blessings.

5. The last and most important step to finding happiness is practising gratitude. This is the most important of all the steps and scientific research has proven the benefits of practising gratitude. Gratitude is a thankful appreciation for what an individual receives. Many of us express gratitude by saying, "Thank you," to someone who has helped us or given us a gift. From a scientific perspective, however, gratitude is not just a word or an action; it is also a positive emotion that serves a biological purpose. With gratitude, people acknowledge the goodness in their lives. Gratitude helps people feel more positive emotions, enjoy good experiences, improve their health, deal with adversity, and build strong relationships.

So the exercise for this chapter is to get yourself into the habit of writing down your goals and to-do list (preferably every day). Ensure you maintain a gratitude journal and every night before retiring to bed; write down everything you are grateful for.

And lastly try to recite the Serenity Prayer by American theologian Reinhold Niebuhr: " God, grant me the serenity to accept the things I cannot change, courage to change the things I can, and wisdom to know the difference between the two." Always remember you cannot control anyone/anything outside of yourself, so control your mind, your words, your body, your thoughts, your habits and your life. And, yes, do listen to The Strangest Secret by Earl Nightingale (again preferably every day).

The biggest problem is that there are so many self-help books and there is no book on how to help someone else. If we learn to help others, we will lead more fulfilling lives. If you want to do something for someone, do it without expecting them to reciprocate it, or appreciate it. Do it because it make you feel better. Eventually someone will witness you do something for others and they will start doing something for others.

Law of practice - You become good at whatever you repeat regularly. It does not matter whether it is good or bad. You become really good at it, if you practice, be it negative thinking or positive thinking, eating junk, or watching Netflix. So choose what you practice.

12 STEPS TO HAPPINESS

THANK
Thank someone and be appreciative toward your colleagues, every single day.

EXPERIENCE
Experience new things, try stuff out, and let people run all kinds of experiments.

GIVE
Give something to another person or make it possible for others to offer gifts.

HIKE
Hike outdoors, enjoy nature, and allow people and escape from the office and the city.

HELP
Help someone who is in need of assistance, or enable colleagues to help each other.

MEDITATE
Meditate and get people to learn and adopt mindfulness practices.

EAT WELL
Eat well, and make good, healthy foods easily available for everyone.

SOCIALIZE
Socialize, relate to other people, and make it easy for colleagues to develop connections.

EXERCISE
Exercise and work out regularly and make it easy for people to take care of their bodies.

AIM
Aim for a goal and get people to understand and realize their own purpose.

REST
Rest well, sleep sufficiently, and enable colleagues to refresh their minds.

SMILE
Smile whenever you can, appreciate humor, and get colleagues to engage in fun activities.

15.
LA FAMILIA

"WE MAKE A LIVING BY WHAT WE GET, BUT WE MAKE A LIFE BY WHAT WE GIVE."
WINSTON CHURCHILLL

So the final piece of advice is to get a dog. Yes, if you want to fix your life, get a dog. If you are not a dog person, then get a cat; if that does not work either then get a fish and, worst case scenario, get yourself a small kitchen garden set up with pots, seeds, etc.

If this confuses you, then let me help you by explaining the various traits of these pets and plants. A dog will shower you with unconditional love and affection, he/she would also be protective of you, whereas the cat will take your affection but will be quite independent. The fish obviously can only be admired from a distance. The plants, on the other hand, require equal attention and if you didn't know they will also respond to your words, music and attention.

Petting a dog can decrease levels of stress hormones, regulate breathing, and lower blood pressure. Research has also shown that petting releases oxytocin, a hormone associated with bonding and affection, in both the dog and the human.

Only with responsibility comes maturity. I owe my dogs – Bruno, Caesar, Buddy and now Snowy – a lot for my sanity and stability. They have taught me the valuable life lessons on learning to enjoy the moment, and not hold on to troubles. As much as I like to believe I took care of them, in reality they took care of me in my most vulnerable moments.

Finally remember to shower your family with love and affection. Your life would be incomplete without the support of your respective families. All of us have taken our families for granted, but without them being around us, like our shadows, we will fall apart. I would not exist without my parents who willingly and sometimes unwillingly let me pursue all my dreams and passions. They gave me everything I needed to live curious. I was fortunate to have in-laws, who supported all my endeavours and encouraged me endlessly.

"MONEY WILL COME AND GO. WE ALL KNOW THAT. THE MOST IMPORTANT THING IN LIFE WILL ALWAYS BE THE PEOPLE IN THIS ROOM. RIGHT HERE, RIGHT NOW."
- DOM TORETTO | FAST FIVE (2011)

EPILOGUE

Throughout history, the world has witnessed empires being wiped out and populations ravaged by epidemics and pandemics. The silver lining has been that these calamities also ushered in an unexpected development within humanity.

The bubonic plague did put an end to medieval socio-economic inequalities and rooted out feudalism. William Shakespeare wrote *King Lear* and Isaac Newton discovered gravity in quarantine. The Spanish flu forced us to develop the public health system and ushered us to invent the modern day vaccines.

The current covid19 pandemic is no different. It is devastating but offers an opportunity to make change. Necessity has always been the mother of invention. Through better collaboration, innovation and resetting purpose, we all can reinvent a smarter and better world. Use this opportunity to reset yourself both on the inside and outside. We spend a lifetime looking outward. Use this opportunity to journey inward, love yourself, heal yourself and reinvent yourself inside out. And for heaven's sake, do not waste this pandemic.

ABOUT THE AUTHOR

Darshan M is a serial entrepreneur who has continuously reinvented himself. From being a topper in school to dropping out of college to becoming a CEO by the age of 32, his journey has been as exciting as a roller coaster ride. His career spans sports, media, fashion and entertainment. He has also acted in a few Bollywood and regional language films. He has served as the CEO of a large public limited company, was the CEO of the title winning IPL team and headed many companies including advertising agencies, media companies and sports management companies.

He currently runs the yoga lifestyle brand Deivee that he co-founded along with Milind Soman. He also runs a sports, media, and entertainment consulting company called PLAY, a production company, Front Foot Pictures, and founded the sports experience company, Sportytrip.

www.ingramcontent.com/pod-product-compliance
Lightning Source LLC
Chambersburg PA
CBHW031434210526
45464CB00005B/2198